Unforgetting
Private Charles
Smith

Unforgetting
Private Charles
Smith

Jonathan
Locke Hart

AU PRESS

© 2019 Jonathan Locke Hart
Published by AU Press, Athabasca University
1200, 10011 – 109 Street, Edmonton, AB T5J 3S8

isbn 978-1-77199-253-4 (pbk)   isbn 978-1-77199-254-1 (pdf)
isbn 978-1-77199-255-8 (epub)   doi:10.15215/aupress/9781771992534.01

Cover design by Marvin Harder
Interior design by Sergiy Kozakov
Printed and bound in Canada

Library and Archives Canada Cataloguing in Publication

Hart, Jonathan Locke, 1956– author.
    Unforgetting Private Charles Smith / Jonathan Locke Hart.
Canadiana (print) 20190066806 | Canadiana (ebook) 20190067586
LCSH: Smith, Charles, 1893-1916. | LCSH: Smith, Charles,
    1893-1916—Poetry.
LCC PS8565.A6656 U54 2019 | DDC C811/.54—dc23

We acknowledge the financial support of the Government of
Canada for our publishing activities and the Canada Council for
the Arts, which last year invested $153 million to bring the arts to
Canadians throughout the country. Assistance is also provided by
the Government of Alberta through the Alberta Media Fund.

For my father,
George Edward Hart,
1914–2018

Who will remember, passing through this Gate,
The unheroic Dead who fed the guns?

                              Siegfried Sassoon

Contents

Part I

Against Remembrance

When I first met him, Private Charles Smith had been
dead for close to a century. I no longer remember
precisely when I came across his small diary in the
Baldwin Collection of Canadiana at the Toronto Ref-
erence Library. With its dark plastic cover and metal
ring binding, it is an unremarkable object—every bit
as nondescript as its author's name. The entries begin
on 5 June 1915; the final one is dated 31 May 1916. Eleven
months or so of Smith's life, pinned to the lined pages,
without past or future.

I had for some time been interested in poetry and
the remembrance of war—not only in the representa-
tion of war in poetry but also, and especially, in whose
poetic voices are privileged in our collective memory.
War poetry typically has an agenda, be it to glorify or
condemn, and implicit in remembrance is always a
forgetting. I first saw Smith's diary around the time
that I was writing a paper for a conference on the
British Empire and the First World War, to be held in

Singapore in February 2014, and my topic concerned, in part, the recruitment of Indigenous soldiers into the Canadian army. These soldiers had, unsurprisingly, been rendered all but invisible in standard, imperial histories of the war: that they be effaced was required by the self-serving logic that undergirds the colonial project, including its wars.

And now here was Charles Smith—who was, I later discovered, firmly Anglo-Canadian, born in Kent. Yet he, too, had been forgotten, along with countless other "regular" soldiers from ordinary families. "Charles Smith" was no one and anyone: in its lack of concrete referent, his name was like all the other names I had seen on gravestones, cenotaphs, and other monuments to the dead.

At first, I had no information about him other than what appeared in the diary itself: "Chas. Smith # McG173 3rd Company Princess Patricia Light Inftry. British Expeditionary Force." And, above the first entry: "Sworn in 5th June 1915." Evidently, then, Smith had received training through the McGill University contingent of the Canadian Officers' Training Corps and had subsequently been sent overseas as a member of the Princess Patricia's Canadian Light Infantry. At the front of the diary, Smith had written:

Please return to
Mrs. E. E. Smith
16 Geneva Ave
Toronto

Was "Mrs. E. E. Smith" his mother? Some other relative? I did not know. Only slowly did my unforgetting take shape.

The first detailed entry is dated Monday, 28 June 1915: "Not much to do today. Had most of the day off. Paraded at 7 p.m. in full marching order. Left Parade Grounds 7:30 bound for boat. Got a good send off. Sailing on S.S. Northland." The diary continues in the same matter-of-fact style. "Was on duty all last Night. Today whilst on lookout 3 bullets struck the chimney just behind me. Weather fine & cool." "Tramp. Weather hot in Day rain at Night."[1] Smith was not writing to express himself—to record his thoughts, his emotions, his opinions. He was simply writing down what happened, in telegraphic style.

---

1 Entries for Saturday, 2 October 1915, and Tuesday, 9 May 1916, Diary of Charles Smith, Baldwin Collection of Canadiana, Marilyn and Charles Baillie Special Collections Centre, Toronto Reference Library, call no. 8vo.

As part of my historical research, I decided to transcribe his diary. In the age of digital scanning, this might seem a peculiar choice, and yet the very laboriousness of the process obliged me to focus my attention on the words I was copying. I continued my work for some time, whenever I visited the Toronto Reference Library, engaging in my own form of archiving, almost like a ritual of remembrance. The voice was his own, full of life—a man in the trenches asserting the individuality of his experience in the vastness and inhumanity of the war. As I transcribed his words, I gradually became alert to their rhythm and cadence, and I found myself wanting to bring forth the poetry I was hearing. As usual, words imprint themselves on me, forming patterns, and a poem begins. In some ways, this poem came fast, as I was merely the scribe to Smith's muse, arranging the score of his composition.

I read the poem to my father, then in his late nineties and still writing poetry himself. When I finished, he asked me a simple question: "Did Smith die, and is that why the diary ends?" His question took me by surprise. I thought back to the unforgettable final entry: "Back at 11 a.m." I was aware that this entry, dated 31 May 1916, was followed by many blank pages—an emptiness that, I realized in retrospect, should have been its own statement. And yet, for some reason, I had vaguely imagined that the young man whose words I had borrowed eventually returned home—or, if nothing else, that his fate was unknown.

The next time I went to the archives, I asked the librarians whether they had any information about Smith. The Baldwin Collection had since moved, early in 2014, into the newly opened, and suitably sleek, Marilyn and Charles Baillie Special Collections Centre on the library's fifth floor. When the collection was moved, the old card catalogues—presumably thought too unsightly—had been hidden away, out of easy reach to researchers, even though not all the information on the cards had been digitized. Another form of forgetting: out of sight, out of mind. A librarian went and fetched the card for Smith's diary, and this is what we read:

```
Smith, Charles, d. 1916.
  Diary, 28 June 1915 - 31 May 1916. 1 v.
Charles Smith was a private in the 3rd
company of the Princess Patricia's
Canadian Light Infantry. He joined the
army on 5 June 1915, as part of the
McGill University Co., 2nd Reinforcement
Draft. He was killed at the Battle of
```

Mount Sorrel, at Sanctuary Wood, 2 June
1916.
  Before the war Smith had lived in
Toronto with his father, Arthur W. Smith,
a painter at the T. Eaton Co. He himself
is listed in the Toronto directories,
1910-15, as a clerk.

  Portrait Picture   Acc. 990-6.

Suddenly, I was overwhelmed with recognition. I had seen this card once before, years earlier. Now memory returned. I had explained that I was interested in biographical information about soldiers who fought in the Great War and had asked the librarians what the Baldwin Collection contained by way of diaries or letters or other such first-hand records. That was how I discovered Smith's diary. But I had completely forgotten what the card said. Indeed, I had forgotten its very existence.

And so my father was right. The diary ended two days before Smith was killed. Since 1916 was a leap year, he had died 363 days after enlisting in the army. He knew that he was sometimes only a few seconds or inches away from death, and yet, transcribing the diary, I had somehow assumed that this was the voice of a man who would survive the battle and come home. He did not.

The card indicated that there was a photograph, and I asked to see it. In the course of my work, my mind had formed its own rather blurry portrait of Smith—a young, generic face, with a look of nobility and determination, my condensation of countless images that I had seen over the years. Now this private portrait gave way to an actual faded photograph, with the sepia tint so popular at the time. A nice-looking young man in uniform, wearing a cap that seemed too wide for his narrow face, his expression serious but uncertain.

The Baldwin Collection had no other information about Smith or his family, but Library and Archives Canada holds extensive personnel records from the First World War, many of which have been digitized. This was how I found Smith's "Attestation Paper," which is dated 5 June 1915, the day he volunteered for service. Recruits were asked twelve questions, to which Smith had responded as follows:

1. *What is your name?*
   Charles Smith

2. *In what Town, Township, or Parish and in what Country were you born?*
   New Eltham, Kent, England

3. *What is the name of your next-of-kin?*
   Arthur Smith (father)

4. *What is the address of your next-of-kin?*
   16 Geneva Ave   Toronto

5. *What is the date of your birth?*
   July 27, 1893

6. *What is your trade or calling?*
   Student (chartered accts' office)

7. *Are you married?*   No

8. *Are you willing to be vaccinated or re-vaccinated?*   Yes

9. *Do you now belong to the Active Militia?*   Yes Q.O.R.

10. *Have you ever served in any Military Force?*
    Q.O.R. 2½ months

11. *Do you understand the nature and terms of your engagement?*   Yes

12. *Are you willing to be attested to serve in the Canadian Over-Seas Expeditionary Force?*   Yes

Below this were two signatures, Smith's own and that of a witness, Guy P. Dunstan. Recruits were then required to make a declaration and swear an oath. The declaration reads:

I, *Charles Smith* [handwritten], do solemnly declare that the above answers made by me to the above questions are true, and that I am willing to fulfil the engagements by me now made, and I hereby engage and agree to serve in the **Canadian Over-Seas Expeditionary Force,** and to be attached to any arm of the service therein, for the term of one year, or during the war now existing between Great Britain and Germany should that war last longer than one year, and for six months after the termination of that war provided His Majesty should so long require my services, or until legally discharged.

The oath follows:

I, *Charles Smith* [handwritten], do make Oath, that I will be faithful and bear true Allegiance to His Majesty **King George the Fifth,** His Heirs and Successors, and that I will as in duty bound honestly and faithfully defend His Majesty, His Heirs and Successors, in Person, Crown and Dignity, against all enemies, and will observe and obey all orders of His Majesty, His Heirs and Successors, and of all Generals and Officers set over me. So help me God.

Both are signed by Smith and duly witnessed by Dunstan. But this is not the end of it. Below Smith's declaration and oath is a statement signed by a magistrate, who certifies that he has "cautioned" the recruit that, were he to provide false answers to any of the preceding questions, "he would be liable to be punished as provided in the Army Act." The magistrate further attests that the "above questions were then read to the Recruit in my presence" and that "I have taken care that he understands each question." His declaration is followed by a final statement from the "Approving Officer," likewise signed and dated, certifying that "the above is a true copy of the Attestation of the above-named Recruit."[2] The document complete, Smith was no longer a civilian.

The war had been underway for barely ten months when Smith signed away his freedom. He was about

---

2 This document can be viewed at "Item: Smith, Charles (MCG173)," *Library and Archives Canada,* https://www.bac-lac.gc.ca/eng/discover/military-heritage/first-world-war/personnel-records/Pages/item.aspx?IdNumber=235643.

seven weeks shy of his twenty-second birthday; he would not live to see his twenty-third. I wondered how, in that moment, Smith understood "the nature and terms of his engagement." The declaration commits him to serve at least until the end of the war—"or until legally discharged." No mention of death here, or even injury, and yet he must have known that he might not survive. Did he sign up because his heart was moved by patriotic spirit, or was he simply doing what other young men were doing? His motives are irretrievable, and they may have been obscure even to him.

I hoped to discover more about the circumstances of his death in the Battle of Mount Sorrel. In one of its collections (RG 150, 1992–93/314), Library and Archives Canada holds records pertaining to the death of service personnel. Volumes 145 to 238, "Circumstances of Death Registers" (also known as the "Brown Binders"), consist of records kept by the Overseas Ministry that specify the circumstances under which someone died and the location of the cemetery in which the person was first buried. These records have also been digitized, and I was excited to think that I might finally learn precisely how Charles Smith died and what became of his body. Excited, that is, until I reached the "Content List" at the bottom of the web page and read the "Important

Note": "Volumes containing names beginning by **Sip to Z have not survived.**"[3] Nothing, of course, about what happened to them.

Suddenly, Smith seemed doubly dead, and not merely because he did not survive, and then neither did the documentation. With the loss of the record, the specificity of his death had also been expunged. I had the attestation paper, to mark the beginning, but I was missing the end. There is no individual record—no death certificate. Browsing at random through other records, I realized, by way of cold comfort, that, had Smith's own survived, it might very well have said no more than "Killed in Action." Some of the forms do contain additional information, but for the most part the entries are terse and perfunctory.

In his *Official History of the Canadian Army in the First World War: Canadian Expeditionary Force, 1914–1919*, Colonel G. W. L. Nicholson provides a detailed account of the battle in which Smith was killed. The Battle of Mount Sorrel took place in western Belgium, on

---

3 See "Circumstances of Death Registers, First World War," *Library and Archives Canada*, http://www.bac-lac.gc.ca/eng/discover/mass-digitized-archives/circumstances-death-registers/pages/circumstances-death-registers.aspx.

a ridge not far east of the town of Ypres, in an area known to military historians as the Ypres Salient. At the time, Allied forces controlled territory to the west of the ridge, including Ypres itself, while German forces were arrayed to the east. From the village of Hooge (roughly due east of Ypres), the ridge curves to the south through Sanctuary Wood as far as a pair of adjacent hills, Hill 62 (or "Tor Top") and Hill 61. Extending west from these two hills is a spur of land, aptly named Observatory Ridge, that affords an excellent view of the area around Ypres. From Hill 61, the ridge continues southward to Mount Sorrel, north of which is Armagh Wood, and then to Hill 60, not far east of the village of Zillebeke (known to Nicholson as Zwarteleen).[4]

At the start of the battle, this crucial area was occupied by infantry units belonging to the 3rd Division of the Canadian Corps—including Smith's regiment, the Princess Patricia's Canadian Light Infantry, which was stationed in Sanctuary Wood. Not surprisingly, advancing German forces were intent on dislodging

---

4 For a map of the battle area as it was on 2 June 1916, see "Mount Sorrel," *Canadiansoldiers.com*, https://www.canadiansoldiers.com/history/battlehonours/westernfront/mountsorrel.htm. The description of the battle provided on this page draws heavily on Nicholson's account.

the Canadians from their advantageous position on the ridge. As Nicholson explains:

> This part of the Canadian line formed the most easterly projection of the Ypres Salient into enemy territory. The challenge to German aspirations presented by this obtrusion was the greater in that the 3rd Division's sector included the only portion of the crest of the Ypres ridge which had remained in Allied hands—a tenure which gave the Canadians observation over the enemy trenches.[5]

Nicholson further notes that, if the Germans were to capture Tor Top, they "would gain a commanding position in the rear of the Canadian lines, and might well compel a withdrawal out of the salient" (148). Indeed, two infantry divisions of the German 13th

---

5 Colonel G. W. L. Nicholson, *Official History of the Canadian Army in the First World War: Canadian Expeditionary Force, 1914–1919* (Ottawa: Queen's Printer, 1962), http://www.cmp-cpm.forces.gc.ca/dhh-dhp/his/docs/CEF_e.pdf, 147. Page numbers are hereafter provided in the text.

Wurttemberg Corps "had for the past six weeks been stealthily preparing just such a blow" (148).

The Canadian forces were aware that the Germans were planning an attack. As Nicholson puts it, "Warnings were not lacking":

During May Canadian patrols reported that German engineers were pushing saps forward on either side of Tor Top. These progressed slowly but steadily in spite of our artillery and machine-guns; and before the end of the month a new lateral trench connected the heads of the saps, now fifty yards in advance of the main front line. The same kind of thing was going on south of Mount Sorrel and at other points beyond. . . . Other indications of forthcoming action appeared in the bringing up of large-calibre trench mortars, and abnormal activity by the enemy's artillery, aircraft and observation balloons. Weather conditions, however, prevented systematic observation of the German rear areas; and the absence of significant troop movements seemed to signify that the looked-for attack was not imminent. (148)

In diary entries for May, Smith mentions periodic shelling, including a piece of shrapnel that hit him in the back. "Felt very nervous," he writes. He cannot possibly have been oblivious to the impending assault.

All the same, Canadian troops were caught off guard when, on the morning of 2 June, heavy German bombardment began. "For four hours," Nicholson writes, "a veritable tornado of fire ravaged the Canadian positions" (148), with one battalion, the 4th Canadian Mounted Rifles, all but annihilated—nine out of ten injured or killed (149). The German fire increased in intensity throughout the morning, and, shortly after 1:00 p.m., "the Wurttembergers exploded four mines just short of the Canadian trenches on Mount Sorrel, and then attacked" (149). Nicholson paints a grim portrait:

> There were brief episodes of hand-to-hand fighting with bomb and bayonet, and where sheer numbers were not sufficient to overcome resistance, the enemy used flame projectors. The machine-guns of Princess Patricia's Canadian Light Infantry and the 5th Battalion (1st Division)—on the left and right flanks—raked the attackers. Though

they inflicted substantial casualties they
could not halt the advance. (149–50)

One of the companies in Smith's regiment was over-
run; a second managed to hold out for some eighteen
hours, "isolated from the rest of the battalions and
with all its officers killed or wounded," while "Patricia
companies to the rear bore the brunt of the fighting."
In Nicholson's description: "Resolute detachments held
successive blocks in the communication trenches, and
the enemy's advance was over the dead bodies of each
little garrison in turn" (150).

Reading Nicholson's account, I began to understand
why the entries in the "Circumstances of Death" regis-
ters are often so laconic. If a fallen soldier lived long
enough to be taken to hospital, or at least to a place
of safety, the nature of his wounds might be recorded
and/or a survivor might later recall what had hap-
pened. Witnesses to the death of those killed in the
chaos of battle, however, might have been dead them-
selves only minutes later. Or, if they survived, they
might not be able to recollect what they saw. Trauma
often blots out memory.

The beginning of the Battle of Mount Sorrel is also
described on the website of Veteran Affairs Canada:

In the fiercest bombardment yet experienced by Canadian troops, whole sections of trench were obliterated and the defending garrisons annihilated. Human bodies and even the trees of Sanctuary Wood were hurled into the air by the explosions. As men were literally blown from their positions, the 3rd Division fought desperately until overwhelmed by enemy infantry. By evening, the enemy advance was checked, but the important vantage points of Mount Sorrel and Hills 61 and 62 were lost. A counter-attack by the Canadians the next morning failed; and on June 6, after exploding four mines on the Canadian front, the Germans assaulted again and captured Hooge on the Menin Road.[6]

---

6 "Hill 62 (Sanctuary Wood) Canadian Memorial," *Veteran Affairs Canada,* http://www.veterans.gc.ca/eng/remembrance/memorials/overseas/first-world-war/belgium/hill62. The memorial is a simple block of white granite, from Québec, on which is inscribed: "Here at Mount Sorrel on the line from Hooge to St. Eloi, the Canadian Corps fought in the defence of Ypres, April–August 1916." During the Battle of Mount Sorrel alone, from the morning of 2 June to the end of 13 June, some 8,430 men were killed, wounded, or reported missing.

The battle would continue until the wee hours of the morning of 14 June, when Canadian forces finally succeeded in recapturing their former position.

Somewhere in this initial slaughter, Charles Smith was killed. He was joined in death that first day by roughly 150 other members of his regiment. But this does not ease the desperation of his struggle or render his death more bearable. Perhaps he was blown apart by an exploding shell, or perhaps he was killed by a bullet and his body then trampled beyond all recognition, on a once lovely ridge overlooking Ypres.

Back home in Toronto, his relatives would not have marked the moment when Smith ceased to be alive; in fact, quite possibly, they were still sleeping. Awake, they would have gone about their business, ignorant of their loss. But they would have been notified, and I wondered what they were told. Was his body ever recovered? Did he have a grave? Curious about his commemoration, I returned to Library and Archives Canada.

Volumes 39 to 144 in the library's collection of death records contain grave registers for members of Canadian Expeditionary Force killed in Belgium, France, and the United Kingdom during the First World War. These registers, which are known as the "Black Binders," include information about the cause and place of death, the date of burial, and the location of the grave. Like the "Brown Binders," grave registers have been digitized, and, in this case, the records from "Small" to "Smith, P. M." have not been lost. When I opened the digital copy, however, I discovered that it can be viewed only a single page at a time and that it is not possible to search the volume—an effort to bury the burial, perhaps. Fortunately, the records do appear to be arranged alphabetically, and by a process of trial and error I was able to locate a record for Charles Smith.[7]

Under "Cause and Place of Death," the record does indeed say no more than "Killed in Action." Curiously, though, the date of death is given as "2/4-6-16." Scrolling page by page through the volume, I noticed several other such entries, such as "14/16-9-16" or "21/22-10-16," but I could find no explanation of the slash other than the obvious one: lack of certainty. So *was* Smith killed on the first day of the battle, as the Baldwin Collection's card indicates, or did he fight on for two more

7 See "Commonwealth Grave Registers, First World War," *Library and Archives Canada,* http://www.bac-lac.gc.ca/eng/discover/mass-digitized-archives/commonwealth-war-graves-registers/pages/commonwealth-war-graves-registers.aspx. "Small to Smith, P. M." is volume 31830_B016643 (RG 150, 1992–93, 314, 122); Smith's record appears on p. 301 and p. 302.

days, only to die on the very eve of the one-year anniversary of his enlistment? I found myself hoping it was the first—not to deny Smith another few hours of life but to spare him the pain of survival. I did not want to imagine him watching as hundreds of others died on all sides, wondering when his turn would come or whether he would merely lose an arm or a leg or an eye or a piece of his face.

No date of burial is listed. Under "Place of Burial," someone had neatly written "Sanctuary Wood, Ypres"— that is, the battlefield itself—but stamped across this are the words "MENIN GATE MEMORIAL." There is also a stamp on the second page: "MENIN Reg FORM SENT 10 2 1925 TO," with "Mr. A. Smith, 16 Geneva Ave., Toronto, Ont." written below, in a different hand. There are no "Particulars"—no information about the circumstances of his death or burial. But then one would not expect them, not in the case of a fallen soldier whose only grave is the Menin Gate Memorial to the Missing.

The registration form was sent to Smith's father while the memorial was still under construction— begun in 1923 and completed in 1927. The imposing structure stands on the east side of Ypres, beside a moat that formed part of the town's medieval fortifications.

Like thousands upon thousands of other soldiers, Charles Smith would have marched along the route on which the memorial now stands, across the moat and on to the woods and ridges several kilometres ahead. Had he been asked, "Are you aware that you may not survive?" he probably would have replied, "Yes." But our death is an abstract idea. He could not have imagined the circumstances in which he would die, much less his final moments of consciousness. Nor could he have known that his name would one day be incised on a block of stone and incorporated into a monument to those whose bodies were never recovered, inasmuch as nothing remained to recover.

Visitors enter the Menin Memorial through one of two soaring arches, one at the west end and the other at the east. At each entranceway is an inscription—composed, no less, by Rudyard Kipling:

TO THE ARMIES
OF THE BRITISH EMPIRE
WHO STOOD HERE
FROM 1914 TO 1918
AND TO THOSE OF THEIR DEAD
WHO HAVE NO KNOWN GRAVE

The heart of the monument is the Hall of Memory, which stretches between the entranceways. Along the hall, on two levels, are seemingly endless lists of the dead, on a total of sixty stone panels, each containing many hundreds of names. Smith's name appears on panel 10, located on the south side of the hall, on the first level, just past the midway point if one is walking from the west. Without a guide to his whereabouts, one might search for days: there are more than 54,600 names.[8]

Stepping inside the Menin Gate Memorial, visitors enter the realm of monumentality—of vast numbers that neatly elide the particularities of human struggle and death. For the purposes of monument, the value of an individual rests on the erasure of that individuality, allowing the person to become a unit capable of increasing a total. Oddly, then, in naming someone, such memorials confer anonymity. Who was "Charles Smith"? And does it matter? He is relevant only insofar

---

8 "Ypres (Menin Gate) Memorial," *Commonwealth War Graves Commission*, https://www.cwgc.org/find/find-cemeteries-and-memorials/91800/ypres-memorial. For an eloquent account of war memorials and the quest for consolation, see Jay Winter, *Sites of Memory, Sites of Mourning: The Great War in European Cultural History* (Cambridge: Cambridge University Press, 1995).

as he is dead. It is hard to think that he earned his place there because in death he had no body—that there was too little left of him to permit identification, whether because he was blown to pieces or incinerated or crushed beneath the panic-stricken feet of others. Who wants to imagine the terror he felt, or the pain? Such thoughts undermine commemoration.

Canada has also claimed Smith as one of its fallen sons, as part of an ongoing effort to repatriate a war not her own. Canada did not choose to go to war with Germany. As Nicholson points out, in 1914, "Canada's constitutional position within the Empire gave her little share in formulating foreign policy and none in declaring war or making peace. She found herself at war through the action of the British Government."[9] This does not, of course, alter the fact that Canadians fought and died in the war. But many of them—especially those who, like Smith, had been born in Britain—doubtless

---

9 Nicholson. *Canadian Expeditionary Force, 1914–1919*, 5. He goes on to quote from R. MacGregor Dawson's *The Government of Canada* (Toronto: University of Toronto Press, 1947), 60: "She had not been consulted; she had herself made no declaration of war; and she had in no way taken part in the diplomatic exchanges which had led to the final catastrophe."

understood themselves as fighting on behalf of the mother country and her glorious empire.[10]

All the same, Canada was swift to focus on commemoration. On 1 July 1917—nearly a year and a half before the war ended—Prime Minister Robert Borden dedicated a site on Parliament Hill for a "memorial to the debt of our forefathers and to the valour of those Canadians who, in the Great War, fought for the liberties of Canada, of the Empire, and of humanity." The original plan was to inscribe, on the walls of this monument, the names of those who not merely "fought" but were, in fact, killed in the course of this noble struggle. There were, however, too many names to be accommodated, and this plan was therefore jettisoned in favour of a Book of Remembrance that would list the names of the dead. The book—completed, ironically enough, in 1942, midway through the Second World War—contains the names of those who died fighting overseas during the First World War. There are 66,655 names. Smith's appears on page 164 of this

10 Indeed, in his diary, Smith recorded his regiment as the "Princess Patricia Light Infantry" (omitting the word "Canadian"), which he identified as part of the "British Expeditionary Force," rather than the Canadian Expeditionary Force.

mammoth roster, sandwiched alphabetically between a Lieutenant Cecil Parker Smith and a Private Charles Henry Smith.[11]

There are now seven Books of Remembrance. These testaments to the slaughter of war reside in a structure known as the Peace Tower—although, more formally, it is the "Tower of Victory and Peace." Peace is, apparently, what follows victory (although it could equally well follow defeat), and, since one cannot have victory without war, one also cannot have peace without war. Moreover, as the books themselves attest, war entails death, and so peace is likewise impossible without the loss of life. To commemorate the dead, however, and thereby celebrate peace, a community must collectively choose to obscure the reality of death. Remembrance requires the transformation of human anguish into heroism, and this is possible only through selective forgetting. In the absence of this forgetting, it would be difficult to lure new generations

11 See "History of the Books," *Library and Archives Canada*, http://epe.lac-bac.gc.ca/100/200/301/ic/can_digital_collections/books/history.htm, where Robert Borden is quoted. The page containing Smith's name can be viewed at http://www.veterans.gc.ca/eng/remembrance/memorials/books/page?page=164&book=1&sort=pageAsc.

into military service. More immediately, in Canada, this elision of death in the service of glorification held out the hope of national unity. "Only the memory of the Great War," writes Jonathan Vance, "could breathe life into Canada."[12]

At the end of my quest, I found myself staring at a page on the website of the Commonwealth War Graves Commission:

Private
SMITH, CHARLES G.
Service Number McG/173
Died 02/06/1916
Aged 21
Princess Patricia's Canadian Light Infantry

---

12 Jonathan F. Vance, *Death So Noble: Memory, Meaning, and the First World War* (Vancouver: University of British Columbia Press, 1997), 11. As Vance observes, Canadians collectively "refused to countenance a preoccupation with the horrors of battle or with the grief of loss," preferring to see in the war "the tool that could weld together the nation" (11). Similarly, in his classic study of the apotheosis of the dead, George Mosse argues that "the cult of the fallen soldier became the centerpiece of the religion of nationalism," in a process whereby "the memory of the war was refashioned into a sacred experience." George L. Mosse, *Fallen Soldiers: Reshaping the Memory of the World Wars* (New York: Oxford University Press, 1990), 7.

(Eastern Ontario Regiment)
Son of Arthur and Ellen Elizabeth Smith, of 16, Geneva Avenue, Toronto.

Suddenly, there was a middle initial, which I had encountered nowhere else. And now I knew that "Mrs. E. E. Smith" was indeed his mother. I wondered whether it was she who gave his diary and photograph to the Baldwin Collection.

Curiously, when I returned to the Baldwin Collection to arrange for a copy of the photograph, so that it could be included in this book, it had vanished. The most plausible explanation seemed to be that it had been taken out for use in a commemorative display in connection with the war's centennial and subsequently then misfiled—a literal effacement, ironically the product of remembrance. Finally, after months of searching, the library staff located it, and, almost as miraculously, Smith's face was restored. The before, I thought, looking at him again, trying hard not to imagine the after.

◆ ◆ ◆

What then of poetry? One thinks of Wilfrid Owen, Hedd Wyn, Rupert Brooke—Owen killed by machine-gun fire only a week before Armistice Day, Wyn fatally wounded on the first day of the Battle of Passchendaele, Brooke dead at sea of septicemia en route to the Dardanelles for the Gallipoli campaign. We think as well of Robert Graves, so badly wounded at the Battle of the Somme that he was reported dead, although, in time, he recovered, and of his friend Siegfried Sassoon, another survivor, honoured for his bravery and yet, by 1917, already a caustic critic of the war. In Canada, we think of Lieutenant Colonel John McRae, teacher, field surgeon, and poet, who died of pneumonia in January 1918, in an officers' hospital in Britain.

Charles Smith was not an officer. Unlike McCrae, he did not write "In Flanders Fields" or earn a page of his own on the website of Veterans Affairs Canada, nor is the house in which he was born now a museum.[13] As far as we know, he never aspired to a career in poetry. His father worked as a painter for a department store, and

---

13 "Lieutenant Colonel John McCrae," *Veteran Affairs Canada,* http://www.veterans.gc.ca/eng/remembrance/history/first-world-war/mccrae.

it seems that Charles hoped to become an accountant. He enlisted in the army, was sent to Belgium, and died. So did thousands of other young men.

When I created a poem from the words in Smith's diary, I did so mostly for myself. It was my way of internalizing his experience. I did not set out to appropriate the prosaic words of an ordinary soldier and elevate them to status of poetry. There was no need: they were already poetry, although perhaps with one exception. Poets—by which I mean people who think of themselves as poets—write with readers in mind and craft their words accordingly. They have one eye on their literary reputation. Whatever else, Smith almost certainly did not conceive of his diary as literature.

Quite possibly, this was private writing, a putting of words on paper with no expectation that someone else would one day read them. Perhaps Smith silently hoped that he would return from the war and that these staccato words would someday serve as an *aide-mémoire*, notes from which stories could then be elaborated. It is a reassuring vision. Then again, whether consciously or not, Smith may have been writing for his mother and father, and possibly for his siblings, if he had any. "Please return to Mrs. E. E. Smith." The request says so much. Perhaps Smith was creating his own memorial, something for his parents to cherish after he was gone—something that, as it turned out, would have to stand in place of his body. He wanted the diary to survive, even if he did not. This could be why he did not speak of his emotions: perhaps he felt that such accounts would be too painful to read. Or to write. Perhaps he could live only by immersing himself in the mundane and immediate and concrete.

What follows is his poem, not mine, although I do think of it as a sort of memorial to his memorial, one dedicated to life rather than death. Smith wrote for those who would continue to live—without him but always remembering him. For once, I want to forget the long lists and massive monuments and instead unforget a single soldier—summon him back to life.

Monday · May 9

Part II

_____

Tuesday May

Wednesday May 31.

The Diary
of a Trench Soldier

A Poem
in His Own Words

June 1915

We did not have much to do today
Left the parade grounds bound for the boat
Got a good send off on the S.S. Northland.

July 1915

Old England at last.
We passed Eddystone Lighthouse,
Sighted a couple of steamships

Trainless through the porthole.
The country is beautiful, but a rotten fog
Came down on us, the church bell ringing

And the echo there.

We received our Lee-Enfields whose bayonets
Were long and can do damage. Folkestone
Is a dead place. Only kids and misfits.

The Minister of Militia
And High Commissioner kept us standing
About for two hours. Tradesmen soak us.

August 1915

Bonar Law inspected us. It rained
And rained.

Nearly everybody had passes for London.
A good assortment of officers
Including some Hindus. I walked the streets

In evening, not crowded. Girls bold
Weather good.

In the British Museum we saw
The Wicked Bible:

Thou shalt commit
And the wicked shall inherit.

Another day: passed chateaux all closed up.
A great country is France. Villages dot
The country. The children are anxious

To know if we are down-hearted.
We passed a gang of German prisoners

Working in the limestone quarry.
Our huts have flowers in the garden.

Nothing doing.
Weather Fine.

A medical inspection that was not.
Train Journey: not so beautiful country
As in England or Normandy.

Carriages rotten. At night I went to sleep
Myself, my leg, my arm. Weather Hot.

September 1915

It is hard to realize we are at war.

A Brigadier-General inspected us
And we showed him how we would take
A German trench. Digging till midnight

Just behind the monastery once under
Shell fire and now only a frame left.
The weather is good for digging.

I saw anti-aircraft fire
Getting right after a plane
That fired more than four dozen

Shots at me. In Dieppe I met a girl.
The Germans bombed Armentières
For an hour.

I saw a great battle in the air. In the night
A fierce bombardment by our lines.
Some scrap: we could hear the machine guns

All at once our plane dived straight down
I thought he had been brought down.
The observer was killed in the air.

We hear that the enemy are going
To flood us out.

                        Nothing to do all day.
What would some think to see us
Eating under the trees? Not the horrors

Of active service.

We are bivouacked in a field
Shaded by trees, slept under the heavens
In good weather.

Nothing much doing all day: we started
A digging expedition. Behind
Our trenches Fritz sent up a flare.

Some are like a parachute, go up
Like a rocket and shoot out and float
Slowly along the lines. Rain whilst digging.

Some night last night.
We had stripped and slept in underwear.
It started to rain and rained all night.

I slept in a pool of water.
Weather rotten.

We are billeted at a barn. Soldiers
Delight: fleas, mice, flies. British and French gains.
Weather fair.

We moved a bit further up. There I saw
A fine dugout that could hold a thousand men.

We patrol the marches: no trenches here.
I was on the lookout: thirteen hours
On and off. Weather cool.

October 1915

The French know about barbed wire-entanglements.
On duty upstairs. I heard the moan
Of the air as the shell cut through.

I was on duty last night. Today whilst
I was on lookout, three bullets struck
The chimney behind me.

The Germans shelled our billets when I was
On duty upstairs. I heard the moan
Of the air as the shell cut through.

We have installed and cleaned a stove sideboard
Have chairs, tables
Feather mattresses. The rain has come.

We have tea, sugar, bacon, cold roast,
Cheese biscuits, bread, jam, spuds, apple sauce, porridge.
Cushing minor thought the waterfall

Sounded like a Zeppelin.

Yesterday, the Germans dropped eleven
Shells, seven of which did not explode.

We had a good joke on Captain Jones. He stepped
Out of his dugout and saw the men
Wearing their smoke helmets. They told him a gas

Attack was on. He ordered all helmets off.
It turns out that chloride of lime had been
Put in the trench and around the latrines.

Poor chaps were overcome. They were so
Excited, they chewed the mouthpieces and have
To get new helmets.

Three to the right and I in front. Schrapnel.
One shot struck a young tree and broke it.

When a shell passes overhead, it makes
A sinister shriek. Macpherson made a splendid
Pudding of dates and biscuits. The weather

Was foggy at night. Late dawn.

The same old thing.

The transports had a time getting down the hill
And one bucked into our billet. We
Loaded stones on to wagons. We had a game

Of lacrosse with shovels and tin of bully
Tied with cloth. The second half was not played.

We took the wood without bloodshed. The weather
Was miserable.

November 1915

Last Sunday was Halloween: we had
Several parcels and celebrated.

Bully Beef works wonders. For a few tins,
We get all the fresh vegetables
We want. A fine sun is out.

We had a bath at a factory. Cushing found
A French family where we go and read and write.
The kitchen was a model of its kind.

In the concert given by our Company,
We had songs, comic and serious,
And a sketch about a veterans' club

In 1964. The weather was fine.

Pay day: we had a grand feed. Roast Beef,
Potatoes, salad, rum cake, apples, café.

The first snow fell about four inches.

Snow again. Same parades.

A hard frost covered all the trees and fields.

Our billet was a big barn. These French people
Speak good English. There are spasms of sun,
Hail, snow, rain.

Nothing doing.

Weather dull.

General Alderson welcomed us
To Canadian Corp. In the evening
We had a great feed on Norman's Christmas

Parcels: ox tongue, chicken and so on.
A good rain.

December 1915

I inspected an old windmill here.
Each had carved his name on the beams.
The earliest date was 1532.

Another date was 1763.
The weather is good.

We had a Battalion route march
For about two and a half hours. We had
A beautiful time wading through the mud.

Nothing much doing.

We went joyfully to Bailleul
Only six miles to take a bath
In a Lunatic Asylum

In a pool sixteen times sixteen
And four and half feet deep
Only about six hundred had been

Before us. In all, we had three baths
One going, one there, one coming back.
Two were in sweat. Weather wet.

Nothing doing.

Same.

Lieutenant-Colonel Pelly said good-bye to us.
He is a splendid man, a gentleman
From his head down. The weather is fine and cold.

I had ordered some Oil of Cedar for my lice
But Selfridge and Company sent O-Cedar Oil
For polishing piano furniture. They

Must think that we have pretty jake trenches.
Nothing doing.

We moved up to the reserves. We have to wade
Through mud ankle deep. The Germans this day
Tried to take Kemmel, but were foiled

By our Artillery. We knew the attack
Was coming off, so when Fritz started
His bombardment, our guns were some

Other place. Next came the gas, but the wind
Was treacherous and blew some of it back.
Next came the Infantry's turn, but

Our gunners were back again and lined
His parapets with shrapnel, so he could not
Get out. The attack ended in the worse

Kind of a fizzle.

Rain all day. Fritz shelled the road and so we turned off
And waded through mud knee deep. We saw
The shells burst close. We could hear the whiz

After we saw the flash of the bursting shell.
We worked till midnight sand-bagging, building up
The parapet.

A fair amount of shelling. We returned through Kemme
The church is badly ruined, with large
Gaps in the tower and also the school.

The weather is still wet.

Christmas Day in the reserves. There was
Holy Communion at Bailleul: we went
In motor transports. Norm and I had

Eggs and chips for tea. The weather is good.

When it does not rain, the sun shines. As a rule
We get four hours sunshine. Work Patrol
At night.

Through Kemmel, we were filling sand bags.
The bullets began to whiz around.
Weather fair.

Pulling up barbed wire, we came home
Soaking wet.

Fritz was shelling the village. One shell landed
Just ahead of us at the cross road. If we had
Been a quarter of a minute ahead, it would

Have landed in our midst. We were issued
With waterproof capes.

We moved off and came back to our same
Old Billet. Jenny was glad to see us,
Also Belgium. We have back our little room

With five table lamps.

January 1916

We had a great New Year's feed. Jenny fixed up
Two chickens with rice, pickles, rolls, tomato sauce,
Plum pudding, cake, apples, cigs, coffee.

A full feeling afterwards. Weather fine:
It rained for about two hours.

Mess orderly today, I had to go
To Flêtre to get up rations. We had
A hot argument about Russia.

Had she done anything in this war?
The weather is good.

Fritz started it. He started to feel out
A battery and put his shells about three fields
Away from us. He put about six shells over

When about a dozen of our Batteries
Opened out on him. It was pretty hot
For an hour. About two dozen whiz-bangs

Skimmed us, just dropping over the barbed wire.
Weather Bon.

An Alleman aeroplane came right over
Our camp. Parts of anti-aircraft shells
Dropped near us. Weather good.

We are on ground level: our trench
Is made of sandbags banked with earth in front.
Instead of digging in, we build up. Weather fine.

Gas alarm: gas was expected, so had to have
A steel helmet handy.

February 1916

We have our cooks up with us this time.
The Glory Hole is on our right.
The trenches are rotten, can be enfiladed

And are only thirty-five yards
From the Germans. Fritz's favourite
Pastime is sending over sausages.

I am happy to say that he never
Gets anybody.

A quiet day. Parlett was killed on patrol
With Perc. Ham. The weather was good.

Corporal Millen was killed in our trench
By a sniper about eight hundred yards away
To our right. The weather was gloomy.

We were relieved by the Forty-ninth.

We came back to Locre
In the Divisional Reserve. We had
A big feed. And we were inoculated

For I don't know what. Whilst in the trenches
We had a Prussian Guard opposite us.
They had some snipers. Their favourite pastime

Was breaking our periscopes.

We have been recuperating
From inoculation. Cold, snow and frost.

Same old thing. Kemmel is a pretty place,
Well wooded with green fields around it.

Out in morning carrying sixty-pound bombs.
Out again in evening for digging.
Fritz sent over about two dozen

Sausages and shells into
The Glory Hole, but did not get
Anybody. He knocked down three parapets.

We are back to our huts in Kemmel.
Yesterday an aeroplane dropped six bombs
Near the chateau. They were probably

After the battery, but it was too close
To be pleasant. They make a terrific
Explosion.

We were out making dugouts. It was
A beautiful day. The sky was full
Of planes and little white puffs of shrapnel.

Two bombs dropped three hundred yards away
From us
And shook the ground where we were.

March 1916

A beautiful day. No Work Party
Was out for drill. We moved off at Two
And we relieved the Forty-ninth

At the Glory Hole amid much rain.
I was on patrol with Morgan to the trenches
On our right. It was snowing all night.

The trenches were up to our calves
In mud and water. This was the hardest night
We have ever put in.

We slept most of the day, making up
For lost time. Heavy shrapnel
Dropped yesterday, which we saw

Bursting, from the trenches.
Very quiet.

The weather was gloomy.

A great day. The monastery at Mont des Cats
Was built in 1026, rebuilt three times.
Payday. I consumed five eggs and sundry

Chocolate.

Heavy shelling. In the front line
The Forty-second and Forty-ninth
Got it badly. Fifty-seven passed through

The dressing station. We were not hit
Although shells burst around us. Weather good.

Heavy shelling in the morning to our right
At Saint-Éloi where we took six hundred yards
Of trenches. I could smell powder and see smoke.

I thought it was a big wave of gas at first.
Miserable weather.

We were relieved in the morning
At 12:30. Fritz was relieved last night.
We have not had much sleep during our three

Days in the trenches. It was a long march
To the train, which took us to near Poperinghe.
We arrived at our huts at 7:30

In the morning. It was a rotten night
For relieving. It was hailing and blowing
Like fury so it was hard to keep balance.

Dark as the blazes. The flash of guns firing
Made matters worse. I found every hole
To be found, including one up to my knee

Filled with soft mud. Our travels were made joyful
By the hail blowing in our face.
We travelled along a trench along a lake

That gave a strange eerie feeling as the waves
Lapped the side of the trench.

April 1916

All muchly disgusted. Canon Scott
Of Montreal came in to see us and made
A great hit with the fellows. He told us last time

He was up at Ypres, he was staying
At a place called Hell Corner. Weather Hot.

We were inspected by a Russian Prince
And also by the Generals Alderson
And Plummer and about a million staff

Officers. We moved away that night.

We were shelled out in the evening
And took to the trenches for about
An hour. None of our chaps was hurt.

An artillery man was killed releasing the horses.
The weather has been good.

I left for Blighty, left Poperinghe for Boulogne
Where I arrived and then sailed,
Arriving at Folkestone, and got to London

Four hours later. I was put up
At the Maple Leaf at 5 Connaught Place.
I had a bath, bed, pajamas, dressing gown

And slippers. I hardly recognized
Myself. The weather was good.

I saw changing of the guard at the Palace
And the Cheshire Cheese, a haunt of Dr. Johnson
And Dickens' Royal Exchange,

The Old Curiosity Shop
Through Petticoat Lane and Covent Garden,
Saint Paul's. I left for Chistlehurst. Weather Good.

I knew the place well. It was easy to find
My way about. When I was a kid,
I used to think the distance between two points

Long. Now find them very short. Miss Foster
Gave me a great welcome. One of the most
Enjoyable meals was a cold supper

The first night here. The weather was good.
Noticed the striking difference between here
And Sanctuary Woods. Here all green

There all shell strewn and battered up.
I saw Mrs. Powell. I enjoy
My meals immensely. Quite Homelike. Weather Bon.

I went to Woolwich. The model housing
For munition workers there was very fine.
I did not recognize grown-ups but knew

All my old chums. Names came easily. Weather same.

I left for London and did a little shopping.
I felt very lonely in evening.
The weather was the same.

I left Victoria Station for Folkestone.
We sailed, a rough passage across, one wave
Caught us broadside, sweeping the deck.

I stayed at Boulogne, then entrained
And left for Poperinghe after midnight.
The weather was wet.

A beautiful day. The birds sang. Easy
Digging. A shell fell about ten, after Fritz had
Put over about thirty high explosive bombs

Within a hundred yard of us. We were almost
Under one of his balloons, and in sight of three.
Hence the shells. We cleaned out the dugout,

Which was in a fearful mess. Bon sleep
As we put in new sandbags.

May 1916

Night Patrol on Hell Street: good digging,
We heard the cuckoo and the skylark.

About four naval six-inches landed
About a hundred yards away. No one hit.
I heard nightingale. The trees were all out in bloom

It is hard to realize that a war is on,
On a quiet day.

A six-inch shell came over. The Forty-ninth
Was badly shelled and had between seventy
And eighty casualties. Fritz put up

A sign that Kut had fallen and that the war
Would be over in two weeks.

Fritz put up a sign that no British troops
Would be in the salient by May 10th.

Work Party: we have had a jake time.
There was hardly any shelling and only
Two casualties in eight days.

One killed. One wounded.

We moved up to supports on Hell Street.
A good dugout. A shell landed near us,
A piece caught me in the back only making

A bruise. I dropped the wine and ran like anything
For the trench. I wanted to get away
From the place. I suffered a little from shock.

I felt very nervous. I am sorry
That it was not a blighty one.

On guard at night—rather wet.
Today is the anniversary
Of Pat's participation in the Second

Battle of Ypres.

Fritz searched for Batteries: he must have put
Over three hundred shells in the morning.
We moved off in afternoon to camp.

Tramp. The weather was hot in day. Rain at night.

I was mess orderly. No mail for a long time.
Weather rainy and cold.